Gifts and Tips

CONTENTS

NATIONAL GEOGRAPHIC School Publishing
Hampton-Brown

Final Blends **nd, nk, nt**

Look at each picture. Read the words.

Example:

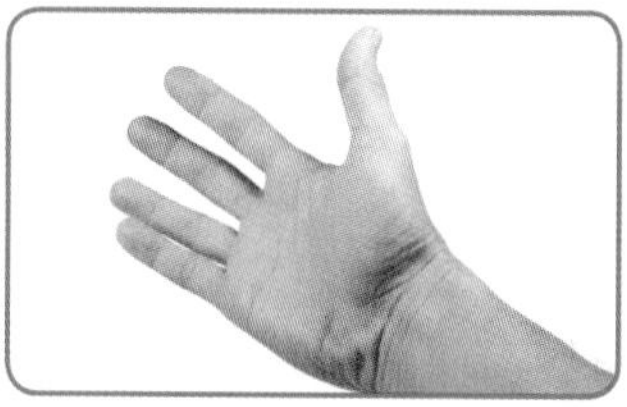

ha**nd**

ba**nd**

de**nt**

ba**nk**

si**nk**

te**nt**

High Frequency Words

- give
- he
- know
- said
- watch
- who

Key Words

Look at the pictures.

Read the sentences.

1. 

2. 

3. 

A Trip to the Bank

1. I did not **know** I had this much!
2. Mom **said** to put it in the bank.
3. **Who** will **watch** it at the bank? The bank man!
4. **Give** it to him, and **he** will lock it up.

Would you spend it or put it in the bank?

GO! **Phonics Games**

NGReach.com

5 Hints for Spending Less

by Hank Dell

If you want to spend less, I can tell you how.

Use my 5 hints for spending less!

Hint 1

Drink tap water.

It's good!

Honk for the Sale

Hint 2

Hunt for a good sale.

And get to it first.

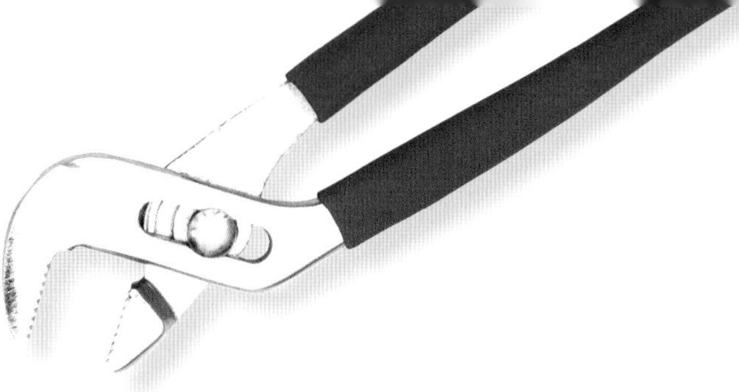

Hint 3

Fix it or mend it if you can.

Hint 4

Who will lend or rent it to you?

Use it. Then give it back.

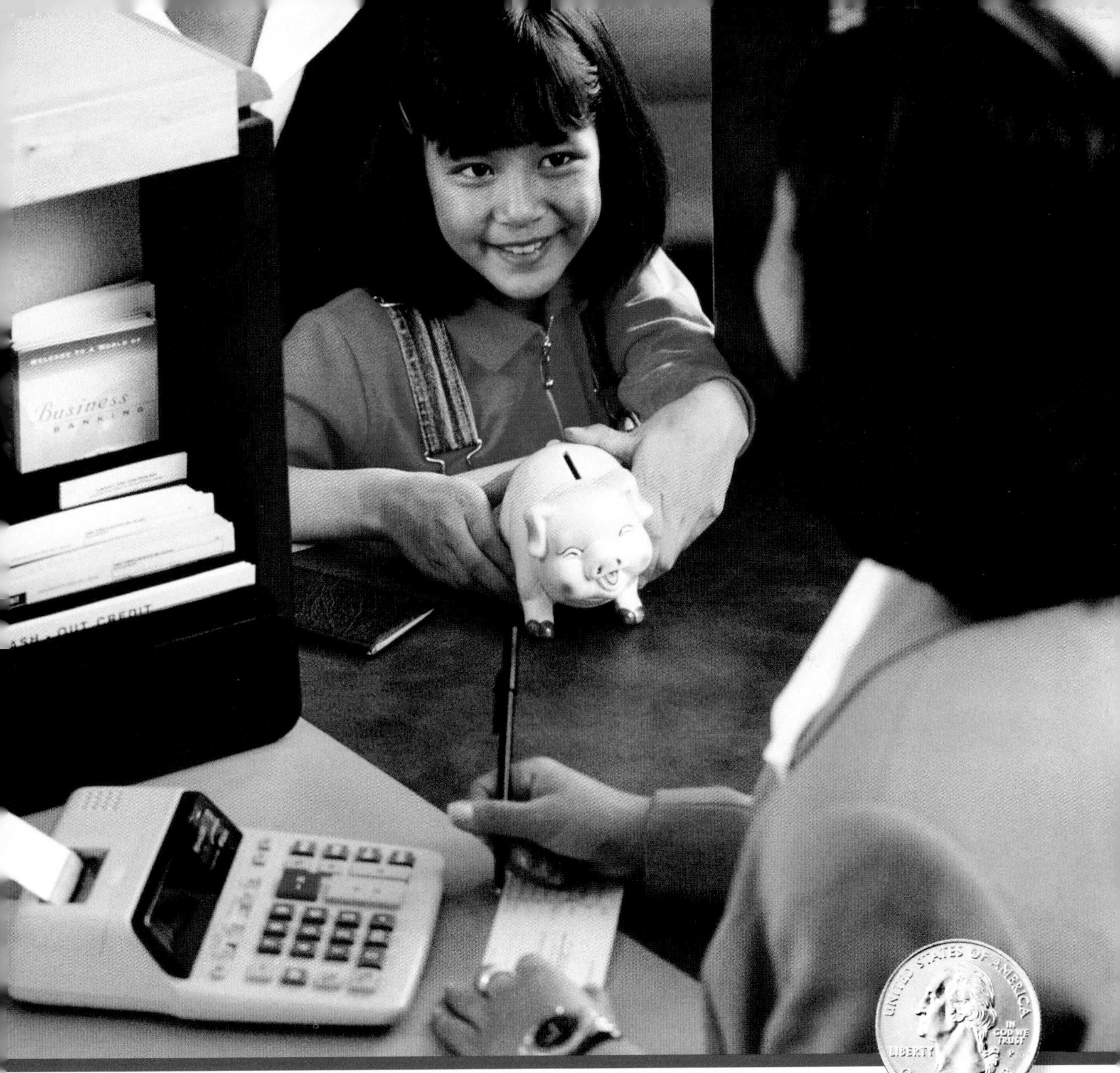

Hint 5

Put what you save in the bank.

You know how to start. Use the 5 hints to watch what you spend!

Final Blends nd, nk, nt

Read these words.

bank	drink	duck	plant
tent	mend	sand	hat

Find the words with **nd**, **nk**, and **nt** blends.

Use letters to build them.

m e n d

Talk Together

What would you spend your money on? Use words from the box above to tell your partner.

I would spend it on a plant and a bank.

More Final Blends

Look at each picture. Read the words.

Example:

la**mp**

gi**ft**

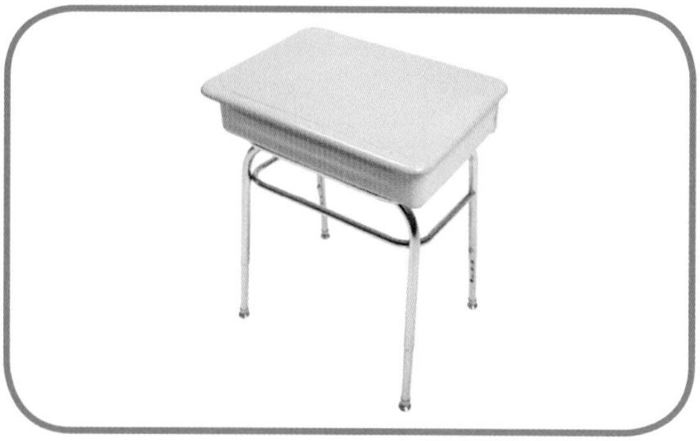

de**sk**

ma**sk**

ne**st**

qui**lt**

High Frequency Words
give
he
know
said
watch
who

Key Words

Look at the picture. Read the sentences.

The Gift

1. Amy will **give** a gift.
2. Do you **know** **who** will get the gift?
3. Dad **said** that **he** will!
4. Amy and Mom will **watch** him open it.

Phonics Games

NGReach.com

The Best Gift

by Kelsey Bruce

illustrated by Huy Vaun Lee

Sam wanted to give Mom a gift.

He had $5 to spend.

Sam went to The Craft Shop. He asked for red and pink felt. It cost $1.

Sam asked for a soft strap. It cost $2. He asked for brass rings. They cost $2.

Sam got home and dumped his stuff out of his bag.

First Sam cut up the felt. Then
he quilted the felt on the strap.

Last he added the brass rings. Do you know what Sam had?

Sam had a belt. Mom said she got the very best gift.

More Final Blends

Read these words.

bag	belt	cap	gift
lamp	quilt	soft	vest

Find the words with blends at the end. Use letters to build them.

s o f t

Talk Together

Would you get a vest or a lamp?

Ask your partner what to get at the gift shop. Use words from the box above.

Tent City

Look at the picture with a partner. Take turns reading the clues. Find what the clues describe.

Find the

1. pink tent.
2. tent that has a quilt.
3. man with a gift to give.
4. tent by a pond.
5. man who will watch Tent City.
6. man who said Scram!
7. one who says Honk!

Acknowledgments
Grateful acknowledgment is given to the authors, artists, photographers, museums, publishers, and agents for permission to reprint copyrighted material. Every effort has been made to secure the appropriate permission. If any omissions have been made or if corrections are required, please contact the Publisher.

Photographic Credits
CVR (Cover) Ray Kachatorian/Taxi/Getty Images. **2** (bl) Milkos/Shutterstock. (br) ukrphoto/Shutterstock. (cl) Soundsnaps/iStockphoto. (cr) Super Stock/age fotostock. (tl) Gualberto Becerra/Shutterstock. (tr) Maria Stenzel/National Geographic Image Collection. **3** (b) Liz Garza Williams/Hampton-Brown/National Geographic School Publishing. (c) Super Stock/age fotostock. (l) Johnny Crawford/The Image Works, Inc.. (r) Leah Warkentin/Design Pics/Corbis. **4** Anton Albert/Shutterstock. **5** (bl) Anton Albert/Shutterstock. (br) Eric Gevaert/Shutterstock. (t) moodboard/Corbis. **6** (b) Anton Albert/Shutterstock. (c) David Sacks/Getty Images. (t) Catherine dée Auvil/iStockphoto. **7** (bl) Anton Albert/Shutterstock. (br) Alexander Maksimenko/Shutterstock. (cl) Comstock Images/Jupiterimages. (cr) Ken Tannenbaum/iStockphoto. (t) Andrjuss/Shutterstock. **8** (b) Anton Albert/Shutterstock. (c) David Samuel Robbins/Corbis. (t) Estelle/Shutterstock. **9** (bl) Anton Albert/Shutterstock. (br) Cappi Thompson/Shutterstock. (t) Jim Cummins/Taxi/Getty Images. **10** (bl) David Samuel Robbins/Corbis. (br) Comstock Images/Jupiterimages. (cc) Anton Albert/Shutterstock. (cl) Jim Cummins/Taxi/Getty Images. (cr) David Sacks/Getty Images. (t) moodboard/Corbis. **11** (t) Liz Garza Williams/Hampton-Brown/National Geographic School Publishing. **12** (bl) Katrina Brown/Shutterstock. (br) Melissa Dockstader/Shutterstock. (cl) Jeffrey Coolidge/Corbis. (cr) AndyTu/Shutterstock. (tl) Kenneth C. Zirkel/iStockphoto. (tr) gaffera/iStockphoto. **13** (b) Liz Garza Williams/Hampton-Brown/National Geographic School Publishing. (t) ImageSource/age fotostock. **21** (t) Liz Garza Williams/Hampton-Brown/National Geographic School Publishing.

Illustrator Credits
11, 21, 22-23 Jannie Ho; **14-20** Huy Vaun Lee

National Geographic School Publishing
Hampton-Brown
www.NGSP.com

Printed in the USA.
Quad Graphics, Leominster, MA

ISBN:978-0-7362-8031-0

18 19
10 9 8 7